Suri & Him

A Paranormal Romance

What The World Needs Now

By Nikel B'nai Dixon

Mohanni Love

SURI & HIM

Let's Jump Right In ....

SURI & HIM

Suri

I was sitting in my parlor braiding my hair with synthetic stretched 36-inch hair in teeny-weeny braids all the way down past my butt with auburn-colored tips very curly. While I was braiding, I started thinking about Nikel and why she left, but I understand that she needed to be a part of baby Suri now. This world we live in is amazing especially when you can view it from a different lens. Smiling to myself I could see Him with the twins while I am doing my hair for 3 days and I get to have a break from life, and I miss my family already and I just in the basement of the castle. Looking at myself in the mirror I smiled and said, " You are a Phenomenal Woman and can do anything you want in this lifetime." I laughed while looking in the mirror because laughing while looking at yourself along with your heart-brain-belly also feeling happy brings in so many good things and happy feels better then sad so being happy is always my go to.

My cellphone pinged and it was a text from Aden and Amir in our group text and they were asking Him, and I could they come to dinner and bring their girlfriends. I laughed because I know about Amir girlfriend, but Aden has a girlfriend now. I texted Him to tell him and ask him which day would be best and he answered me saying how Aden now have a girlfriend now we both shared laughing emojis then he said Friday night and they could stay if they want. I told him ok, and I agree also it gave me time to finish my hair. Then He texted to me " I Love you baby" I answered back " I love you and miss you Baby." I sat the phone back down picked up a spaghetti sized piece of hair and started braiding with a smile on my face to being in that good stuff to my life. I should be finished my braids in the next 24 hours. I love hiding while I do my hair those are the little things that keep Him always wanting and wondering about me which is very important in a relationship. I know it is time for us to start running this world but to me the most complicated will be our people the black people.

SURI & HIM

They always pointing fingers and forgetting that while they are pointing there is a thumb pointing up to GOD and then three fingers pointing back at them and to me that means that they need to find other ways of expressing themselves because so far, the majority of them are killing one another-jealous of one another-hurting-one upping and more then they wonder why they are being treated as so. Forget about the past and all people need to bound together and move into the "NEW WORLD" we are trying to develop. We need to fix all this baffling that goes on about slavery and what we deserve and move forward being better human beings and then it all will fall into place . I am so happy to have a man like him by my side and many times I have to walk behind him because he knows way more than I and he is well suited to take care of business in the correct manor but me on the other hand I want to curse people out and get crazy and I can't do that being a Queen even though so many people need that. I can hear Him laughing so I said, " Stop Ear hustling Babies." He said, " Nah baby you are right."

I was sitting and thinking about how my people worry about what other people got as far as their money-clothes-assets and then if another black person is doing great things in life there are some blacks who sit back and lurk-wait to catch them in their shit or wait for them to do something wrong. I have watched this with my closest family members who sit and watch you and wait until you do something or say something then they give you that " Gotcha moment."

If all the races can bound together then they could learn so much from one another now I would never think or say that other races don't go through some of or the same things because when I talk I am talking about my own race because that is what I am and what I know but I just think that black people have wasted so many years humming and having about why the white man do us wrong " Well do black people ever think that white people are treating us as we treat us shit they are learning from the best so how wrong are they to have this view about the black race". It is a shame that sometimes it can bulk us all up together but that is how life is no matter your race we all do it so the world need to get it right by removing that race shit and just trying to love and stop worrying about other people and what they got and join them so then we can work together to heal the earth.

I believe the 5th dimension will consist of various races who have kindred spirits who doesn't see color because I must admit my best ships came from white people or other races my own people sat around to find what was wrong with me or they were jealous, so I became a loner especially after my family did it. This shit is real but one thing for sure is I got Him-kids-my babies-and even Lizzy who come from Love we don't sit around watching and waiting for one of us to fuck up! We work together to help one another grow.

SURI & HIM

      The past definitely should be in some kind of History books that people should want to look up but we need to start books titled " THE NEW HISTORY BOOK" and start all over comminated with so many different nationalities who honestly made inventions and did not steal them-helped people be better I am so tired of the past because truth be told teenagers today don't give a fuck about what happened years ago and they are our future so moving forward it's them who we have to bridge the gap with I don't even know if the majority of the adults could be helped.

      When I do take the time to turn on the news our teens are killing one another a=but we could bridge the gap by lowering the age for them to work to 15 years old these teens can work a computer better than adults. Let them be able to make a decent salary and work for companies like IBM or even Tesla . Adults worry about their behavior at work but the adults at work at more immature than many teens. This old school world can't work moving forward or only the people who can elevate to 5D will be a part of this kind of life and world. There will be peace, but nobody is perfect so when someone trip up and make a mistake, they will be able to go right back to their 5D status because it is inbred in them. I turned to look in the mirror at my braids which are very beautiful.

      I remember when GOD gave me all the keys and I can't even tell anyone all of them not even my hubby, but I can see that the more I try to council my family who watch the tube all day long and they don't know that they are being programmed not to go to 5D see the GOD knows who will be an asset to the 5D realm and who will be a liability so right now everyone is going through a test each and every individual and it starts with... I just lost my train of thought hmmm I guess I almost gave some of my keys. People ask me how do I braid my hair like this and I always smile and say, " I think while I braid my hair, and this is the outcome of my thoughts." I really don't know but I thank God every day for our personal relationship, and I thank him of the bad things I went through growing up because look at the phenomenal woman I have become.

SURI & HIM

My phone pinged again, and he sent me a picture of our babies sleeping they were hugging each other sleeping cheek to cheek awe sooooo cute I love them so much. I text back asking him can we sleep like that from now on he sent me back laughing emojis. After looking at the text I opened my internet app and to look for a pair of candy panty g string for me I found them, placed the order, and expressed it to get it in two days. I texted him back and invited him to meet me at this hotel I was looking at located on Central Park West in Midtown Manhattan. I booked the room then I told him to meet me there just for one night I miss him and like I always tell myself that "I will always be exciting to him" at least I am trying.

I woke up this morning and finished my braids then braided the ends together really tight then dipped them in boiling hot water and squeezed them with a cloth. I ran me a nice hot steam bath took my extremely long braids and let them hang outside of the tub while I laid on my bath pillow to rest. I texted Lizzy asking her could she please watch the twins for one night while we got out, she sent me laughing emojis telling me that he already asked her. I also told her that I pumped extra breast milk, and it is in the small new freezer on top of the meat freezer she liked my message meaning ok. I took out my razor and shaved every place on my body that had hair accept my head of course. I never did this before with him I wonder how he would like this. People say that we have hair in certain places for certain things and ok just like a baby boy is born uncircumcised and that must be the way men should be but the majority of people circumcise their sons so me shaving my vajayjay is my choice for the moment so I will not guilt trip about it. Lizzy text me telling em I just got a delivery and him. I told her to leave my package by the door on the table so I can grab it on the way out.

I arrived at the hotel around 6:35pm and then texted him the hotel room number, I ordered sweet red wine-chocolate covered strawberries-bourbon. I took off my clothes to try on my candy panties and what was so cute was they came with a candy necklace-bracelet-anklet-and the panties I bit one off the string to see if they taste the same. After I put it all on, I took my braids to cover my tits which was extremely sexy. My belly was still soft from the pregnancy as a matter of fact my whole body have become very soft. This is the first time we had sex since the babies I just hope that my body changing doesn't turn him off. I must get my ass back in our gym every morning to get tight ass I can but the women in my family have no elasticity to their skin after kids. Look at my mind having all these thoughts while looking at my beautiful self in this full-length mirror.

SURI & HIM

    I took this cherry skin oil I made from scratch and applied it to my entire body to give it a glow. I stood up and was admiring the room poured me a glass of that sweet red then I was leaning up against the wall looking at the lights from the New York City Night life when I heard the door lock click . I haven't seen my baby in so long, so I turned around and stood there made sure my braids were covering my tits and when Him walked into the room he stood there with his mouth open then smiled at me I took my eyes and let them go all the way down to his crotch and I stared at it until I saw it rise from under his pants. Then I side smiled at him then slowly sauntered over to him until I leaned into his hands holding my face to passionately kiss me then his hands went down to my ass, and he began to squeeze my cheeks softly one in each hand then he kind of moved them together. I know he wanted me to twerk for him I understand his notions. I reached behind me and grabbed his hand walked him over to the bar to make him a bourbon then he sat down and kept staring at my ass. I handed him his drink then turned around and started twerking for him he reached up and started smacking my ass. Then I sat down on him to give him a lap dance he laid down on the bed. I stood up and slowly turned around then kneeled down in front of him and took out his dick then pulled off his bottoms. I took both hands and started massaging the insides of his thighs softly reached to get my cherry oil and started rubbing it all over his inner thighs until I rubbed all the way to the tip which is his heart, and I kissed the tip with my eyes closed and moaned just enough for him to feel the vibration from my mouth then I sucked on him for a few minutes. When I stood up, he looked at me and told me how beautiful my braids were and I was, so I said Thank you to him. I stood and placed both hands to pull down my panties, but he stopped me and laid me down opened my legs wide leaned in between my legs and asked me could he taste a piece of candy and those words turned me on so much that I could feel heat flowing to my sweet spot. He licked the whole panty from the bottom to the top and started telling me good it taste. He took his long finger and lifted the panty a little to put his finger under to move the panty to the side and when he saw I had no hair he looked back at me and said, " Baby Oh baby." Then he took both hands, popped the panties off and then started licking my sweet spot all over he actually dove in and sucked me like he was ravenous until I exploded, and it felt nonstop. Then he stood up on both knees with his hard dick in his hand and he could barely fir inside of me, but he took his time until he got in and while he was loving me, he started telling em how my body feel so good, and he loves my bodies new texture. He started with this pillow talk and he never really did this before, but we had sex-made love-fucked for four hours and his last explosion I could feel his pulsation and it was still strong. He kissed me nipples then told me that he love me so much and thank you for being special for him.

SURI & HIM

      We arrived back home, and I felt like we were even more in love then before. When we went to our bedroom. We told Lizzy that we will be there to pick up the twins in a few she told us to take our time. Him was sitting in the chair texting back and forth then he looked at his watch then texted again. I went to the bathroom to change but I notice he didn't. When I came out of the bathroom, he came over to me and then asked me could he go out with the guys. I jumped up to kiss his lips and laughed then asked him could I dress him? He laughed and said you gonna out a chicken suit on me or something then I said nope I got a surprise to you the samples came in two days ago. I went to eh room next door to us and waved him to come with em and when we walked in there was a wardrobe of clothes that I designed for him all of his clothes had a small logo of the Himsur Crest and in the eye was a colored stone to match the fabric. There were hats-hoodies-sweats-jeans-sneakers. He sat in a chair, and he laughed telling em that he can't wait to see what my taste is for him in clothes. I took out this yellow Angora Sweater with a matching Angora thin skull cap and each of them had the Himsur crest with a yellow stone in the eye. He leaned into me and gave me a kiss telling em how he loved every piece, and he will wear that yellow get up. Then he asked me why wasn't I upset that he was going out I told him that I am not your mother I am your wife baby. I want you to go out and have fun you don't always have to have fun with me only and I know you need a break. Then I paused then added " and anyway you know better than to do anything you are not supposed to do because then I have to get you babies." Then we started laughing at me while he took an outfit off of the rack. When we walked back into the bedroom, he told me that he is not leaving until after we eat dinner with the twins and their girlfriends.

Aden & Amir Dinner Date

The doorbell rang and we could hear the twins talking to Lizzy introducing their girlfriends. Lizzy took them to the large dinner room. We heard the twins ask for the babies Lizzy texts us to ask us if it was ok. We told her yes and the babies will be with us for dinner and until further notice. Lizzy obliged.

When we entered the room, the girls stood up they were beautiful Amir girlfriend was Jamaican and so petite and about 4'11 in height. Aden Girlfriends had ginger hair down her back and was Caucasian beautiful and she was 4'9 it seems and very petite. We walked over to them I gave them a hug and him welcomed them with a handshake then we both sat down across from them on the couch. Aden & Amir was there silly self as always and the energy from these girls seemed all good, but Amir girl look like if he step wrong, she will get crazy. Him and I was laughing at them the whole time because they have grown up tremendously. I asked then what were their future plans Aden girl name was Amari and Amir girl name was NorayNae. So, Amari said she owns her own digital company and bakery and NorayNae works hard double shifts as much as she can. I liked them both but of course everything is always good in the beginning Amir been with his girl for longer than Aden, so I know her better. The food was all laid out like a party with Italian food, and we all got up and went to the table to eat. Him and I put the babies in their chairs. The twins were talking about wanting to embark on the Christmas gift him gave them to start their own businesses so they asked Him could they come one day next week to sit down with him. Him looked at them with a smile and told them of course and how he was waiting for them to ask. I was looking at the girls and I saw a vision of a website, so I told everyone that I had a vision that I started a business around them it was a business called " Ginger & Spice and Everything Nice." The business was online and sold fresh ginger-ginger snaps-ginger candy-ginger syrup and a bunch of spices by the pound for seasoning food. We all laughed but then I asked them what did they think about that and they both smiled and said it sounds really nice sooooo. I took my phone and started the paperwork on it. Him was looking at me with his mouth open then he whispered, " Are you a Business making Machine." I laughed then whispered " These businesses come from God, and he told me that they are everlasting. They flow all day abbacies." He laughed and we kept on eating.

SURI & HIM

After dinner they asked could they stay I looked at Him and asked Him could they stay, and he said yes then I added but no baby making please the girls said out loud oh no never. I twisted my lips at them and said yeah okie dokie. We went upstairs and I got Him clothes together laid out then I slipped something in his pocket. I went to get his heavenly cologne. While he went to take his shower then when he came out of the shower, he was telling me how shocked he was that I was not upset he was going out and I was helping him look good. I laughed then said yes babies you represent me when you go out and you must look and smell delicious. I trust you and I am confident within myself. He started at me then he reached to get dressed. I sat and watched his get dressed all the way down to his feet. Then when he picked up his keys I stood up and asked him could I pray over him for safety. He smiled then said of course then we held hands and I started to pray and when we both said Amen in the end. I bent over and pointed my finger at his crotch and told his other head to behave and be a good boy. He held his stomach and laughed at me then he kissed me he was walking out of the door then she stopped turned around while standing in the doorway and he said, " Oh yeah baby I put my tracker on, and I will be meeting the guys at Gilleos's Sports Bar in Midtown Manhattan." I said oh okay then I reached to put the babies on the bed so I can give them a bath then he came back and told me to make sure that I press the recorder to play the tapes with Him speaking French so they can start to learn foreign languages. I looked at him and said, "Well alright Brotha." He laughed and left.

I bathed the babies, and they were laying there so cute and happy, so I started playing the tapes and I went to my closet to turn on my old phone to start to transfer numbers over because it's time to get down to business and Life Always goes On No Matter What.' I turned it on then I remembered the babies I forgot to put a pillow on each side of them and our bed is very high I can't have then fall Him would kill me if that happened." After I placed the pillows, I stayed with them and was repeating the words to them until we fell asleep.

When I woke up it was 3:30am so I went to take the twins one at a time to their nursery then I went to lay back down and go to sleep.

SURI & HIM

    I was sleeping really well when I heard the bedroom door close, I opened one eye and, in the dark, saw Him taking off all of his clothes then he had something in his hand it seems he turned me over fast then ripped my gown off he looked pissed off. I stayed quiet because when a man is pissed off a woman's words can cause him to lose it, so I decided to enjoy the moment. After I was naked laying on my back he cut on the light and held up the condom I slipped in his pocket then he opened it and put it on then proceeded to make love to me and the whole time he was talking telling me that " I better not ever put a condom no were near him unless I want to use it with him then he continued telling me that he is not a cheater he been there and did that years ago and he only want me and nobody else I satisfy him in every way. I had an orgasm that felt amazing from his energy then he really pumped deep inside of me while he told me to answer him that I will never do this again. So, I said " Ok babies no problem." I enjoyed that so much I might to do it again for the rush I Really Love my husband. I rolled over and gave him kisses on his face while he went fast to sleep.

    We woke up to the cries of the twins from the Himsur baby monitor. We both opened our eyes and looked at the camera and they were all on each other crying. I told Him that he can go back to sleep because he had a full night yesterday, he blew me a kiss and laid back down. I ran quickly to the twins and started talking to them telling them it is okay, and mommy is here then they looked at me and I told them that daddy was resting, and he will be here soon. I turned on the recorder so they can hear their daddy voice and they stopped crying then I we heard Him through the baby monitor say " Ummmhmmm" I looked at the monitor and laughed. I turned around because I could feel someone there and it was the twins and their girlfriends telling me I can go back to bed, and they will watch the twins. I looked at the monitor and before I could ask Him answered them and said " thank you ". So, I kissed both of my babies and ran back-to-back and dove atop of my man he hugged me-held me and then we went back to sleep.

SURI & HIM

When we woke up, we saw that they were still in the babies nursery taking care of them then I heard Amir girlfriend ask why did I always ask Him when I make decisions about everything. Amir turned to her and said, "because actually that is the way it should be they both consult with one another religiously." She said Oh then Amir said loud to her OH! I looked at Him and he put his fist up and said yes Amir tell er. They could not hear us, but we were laughing at them.

Later that day we decided to sperate him hung out with the boys and I hung out with the girls. I took them shopping to the W Mall in Westchester. When we came back home, we all were sitting in the lounge talking then NorayNae asked me why do I always ask him for permission or let him make all the decisions. I looked at her smiled then told her that the way the world have been running in these years the woman have taken all control from the man so people have the habit of always asking the woman when it comes to anything and very rarely the man but one thing for sure is if questions are ever directed to Him, he definitely will turn to me and ask me like I do to him . In our relationship we love one another so much that we make sure that we never leave the other person out no matter what it is and honestly, I love having a man in my life who can lead all the time and I lead sometimes because all that leading, and decision making is exhausting and if he ever make decisions without me then I know he thought about it before he made it. See today's woman especially the black woman I can speak about because I am a black woman have been leading so much that the black man have climbed into a shell and have now given off this wimpish energy but what I think is going on is that they are hunting for the right match for them and sooner or later all those woman who want to lead in the relationship will get exactly what they want and that is to be alone because truth be told with that leading energy what do they need a man for his money? And after a while he will stop that flow too then what. I used to feel like I wanted to tell woman to love their man more or to change their present energy but I knew that I could not change that so I decided to sit back relax and watch their show and I knew that one day I would find Him the man for me, and I will treat him like a king because since he is my match it can only be given back to me. It's All About Love NorayNae and when you see that love is no longer in your relationship then it is time to leave because time can never be gotten back but only in a memory and what good is that really.

SURI & HIM

Now I did not raise you so my idea of how to treat a man might not be how you were raised to treat a man but one thing I know for sure is that if you want your man to make you happy it starts with the treatment you are dishing out to him. Always use sweetness and sweet tones always do things to melt his heart and if he ever fumble because he is not perfect then you lift him up and wipe the dirt off his knees and help him do better because in the long run you will always win with him and sometimes you might have to walk behind him-beside him-in front of him but always be open to that walk behind him and let him take care of the shit but if you have to intervene then you do that without a doubt respectfully never take his manhood from him when you start to speak but one thing for sure you and him have to always make each other look great in public never ever discuss your downfalls . Girlie poo I have a plethora of information to help mold you into A Real Boss Woman, but you have to be eager to want to learn and it takes a special woman to be able to uphold all that I just told you. None of this is hard the first thing you have to do is reprogram what your mother told you or how you saw your mother treat your father then that way you are making your relationship thrive doing it your way but only if you can relate but if not, life is full of learning experiences and situationships and choices. You are still young and who knows who you will marry but Amir and Aden is watching how their mother treat their stepfather and how happy we are so I am almost sure they will want the same kind of respect from their woman. I can only keep it real with you and remember money isn't everything Love, and respect is everything. Lastly, I am not telling you to do what I did I am answering your question. NorayNae was sitting there staring at me with her cute little face and Aden girlfriend was shaking her head yes with everything I was saying (hmmm).

Him walked over to me and kissed me then he whispered in my ear " baby those words were epic, and you should share that with other women." I took my finger to tell him to come closer again and I whispered in his ear " I could only teach young woman because so many women have been tainted by their unhappy ass momma, so the disease is all over their mindset." He looked at me and smiled then I said Baby Suri and Baby Him is gonna be something else.

Him turned to me then said, " Oh yeah I forgot I saw your friends at the Sports bar you know Nikki and them and one of them asked for my autograph, so I gave it to her then I kept right on with my boys." I told him ok then I kept laughing and talking with the girls.

SURI & HIM

The kids left and went back to my Condo to stay I guess this is the next surprise that Aden and Amir will tell me, but I will wait until they do, or I will do a pop up late one night. We put the twins to bed and what amazes us is how they talk baby talk to each other then they wrap their arms around each other than fall fast to sleep. Then we walked holding hands all the way to our room to take a relaxing hot bath together. We both laid our heads on our bath pillow and was quiet enjoying the serenity of the bathroom. We heard a phone ping, but it was different not like our regular phone ping that we programmed our phone to make. We continued to rest then we decided to get out because we almost fell asleep. After drying off we went to bed spooning then the ping again, so I sat up and looked over to him side were both our phones sat and they both were off then I remembered I left my old phone in the closet on my dresser, so I told him it was that phone . I go tup and went to get it and when I picked it up there was a text from Nikki with a photo, so I downloaded the photo, and it was him with this woman standing very close to him and from the angel of the picture he looked like he was enjoying her company. So, I walked back to the bed, and I handed him the phone and he laughed then said this is the girl I was telling you about your friend. I said I know babies but read the words on the bottom of the picture from Nikki . When he read the words, they read " see Suri I told you that he will always have that cheating in his blood don't trust him." He looked at it then said, " baby this is big bullshit." I got up and went to sit down to pump my breast because they were full but then I stood up and let the milk run out because I was so pissed off over Nikki bullshit text, I don't want that anger to be in my breast milk that I give my babies. I really believe that when you breast feed your babies you must be extremely happy because you are sharing a piece of you to them. Him sat up staring at me then he started to explain so I stayed quiet, and I asked him to get dressed and lets take a walk on the grounds. He looked hesitant at first, I was already dressed in a sweatsuit with my hood on no panties or bra and my breast milk was flowing making wet spots. He got up slowly I leaned on the wall by the door waiting patiently for him to get dressed . After he got dressed, we walked out of the back door side by side. He kept on trying to explain he was really scared but it was never him I was upset about I just can't talk right now .

SURI & HIM

We walked and stopped over by the weed field . I opened the gate then closed it behind us we both went to sit down on the bed we have there I walked over to cut off one of the strongest strains that we carry. I sat next to Him and started breaking it up into the crusher then grinding it in mt hands . Him sat up against the headboard and was just watching me. I opened the wrap and started spreading the weed inside evenly the I started rolling. I handed it to him then I rolled mines. After we lit them and started smoking, I told him that I needed to calm down and this was the way I only knew how because Nikki and those chicks were tryna make me jelly babies. He shook his head and said he knew that but didn't know at the time.

I told him that he is a star so I expect that from women, and I don't care about that but the ones who know me and I know they tryna fuck with me I did not want to do this, but I want to show you babies what I can do to people I was born with this gift that I don't use but they pushed me. Him sat up and said wait baby think first I looked him in his eyes and said I already thought. I told him to observe so I took the phone out of my pocket, and I text Nikki back and it read "

Suri

Hey Nikki thanks for that and did you like the sweater I designed for my baby I got his clothes ready for him to wear that night. Anyway, sweetheart enjoy your night and I Love you darlin.

Nikki

Oh, ok girl enjoy your night.

We both heard a phone ping, and it was his phone from them telling us to meet them at the landing strip now. So, I got up and we left and went to the landing strip. In about 3 seconds after arriving, they zapped us up.

Meeting With Them

    There we were siting on the beds and all four of them were there and was staring at me. I was so high that I really did not give a fuck at this point. The lady started laughing and then she asked me was I sure I wanted Him to see what happens when people push you to the edge especially when you are a good person and always happy. I looked at her and shrugged my shoulders. Him was sitting there just looking back and forth at her and I. then she turned to Him and touched his hand and said hello I could hear the whole convo I got my shit together now my mind is ready. So, she told him that ever since I was a little girl in BC, I would still love my abusers or people who hurt her even till this day but when she tell them that she loves them, and she let go completely what they have done or doing to her then Suri gives the person to GOD he deals with them as he see fit but Suri can't intervene, she must walk away. Him looked at Suri. Then we saw the movie screen again on the walls and it was Nikki and the girls laughing and talking about Suri really bad even planning what they were gonna do next and what they were planning was really bad . I looked at Him with water in my eyes and said I was only a good friend to them every time I get a friend, they be so jealous they plan to hurt me, and I don't even see it coming. The lady turned and placed this monitor on my chest and then she said look at this you still love these people, and this is why then Him said what do you mean this is why. Then the lady changed the subject then asked about the twins and we both smiled telling them about the babies. They told us that the twins are intuitive and if anyone ever hold them and they cry it definitely is a clear sign that they know the persons heart. Then I told them that all babies have that gift then one of the men said but Suri your babies have your gift of protection so if a person means harm the person will be dealt with by the spiritual realm. We looked at each other and we were so high it was crazy. The lady gave me some pills that remove the weed from my system in an hour so then I can pump my breast then she told me I was smart about not pumping milk when I am upset only when I am happy. Then they told us goodbye, and we were both standing on the strip.

    When we went back home, I took a shower my breast milk was flowing like crazy then I put on my nipple cream and breast pads along with my ugly bra for breast feeding and we went to sleep we had a long night.

SURI & HIM

When we woke up, we went to check our emails because it was time for work. Then my phone dropped down Breaking News and I saw that last night 4 girls were in a tragic car accident then they showed their faces, and it was Nikki and the girls. All I could do was cry Him just sat there with his mouth open. I was crying telling him I wish I could hate so then things would not happen to people but my heart only loves even when I am disappointed in what person has done to me, I still love them.

I looked at Him with my eyes red from tears and told him that one of the keys that was gifted to me was to keep love in your heart at all times and let the universe or whomever they are take care of your battles because these battles on earth are not ours when we do good things, and we help people, so we are supposed to love who hurt us and give them to the heavens. Him came over and held me while I cried, he waited until I got all my tears out it was like he knew exactly what I needed. I needed him to hold me and never let me go. In all my relationships the times that I cried I was always just looked at but Him knew when I needed him the most. While wiping the snot from my nose in a shaky voice I started explain to him that I know he is a celebrity, and I would never come in between fans who love him because he probably could save someone life or make someone's day just by giving them his autograph or and kind words. He took his hand and pulled me close to his chest while I continued to cry then the babies started crying, we both looked at the monitor then him said " everyone's crying tonight huh and we laughed he came and gave me a kiss then he reached out his hand and we went to the babies room.

SURI & HIM

Him

    We have been going through so much lately after we put the babies back to sleep, I went to my office and Suri went to go talk to Lizzy and Christopher while they were cleaning out the fridge. I decided that we need time away to cleanse. The doorbell rang and when Lizzy opened the door it was both Suri and my mother and they both were pissed off they walked into my office I was siting there looking at them. Then Suri marched in and stood by my side resting her arm on my shoulder while I was siting down. Our mothers was telling us how and why we haven't called them to come help us with the babies and how upset they were about that. Suri whispered in my ear telling me how cute it was watching them together ready to fight us over their grandkids. I love the fact that my wife knows when to give me the lead because this one I am going to love. We both was watching them go back and forth yelling at us and agreeing with one another. I started typing on the computer while listening to all the rhetoric Suri was watching the screen, she saw me book a private island space by the ocean in Hawaii for a week all inclusive with a beautiful cabana along with a bed inside and outside for us to chose where we want to sleep. Daily massages for the both of us and more.

    I waited until they finished then I walked over to them and gave each one of them a hug individually then I text Lizzy and told her to bring the twins to my office. When Lizzy walked in with them, We both picked up a baby kissed them and then we handed them over to our mothers. I told them that they are right we should have called them, and we were wrong then I told them that we are leaving right now to Hawaii for a week feel free to stay and take care of your grandchildren just meek sure they listen to my foreign language tapes at night with my voice and then Suri says oh yeah, I made tapes too we all started laughing and I asked Suri should I listen to them first Suri said nope trust me my tapes are good too. We all laughed kissed our mothers and we walked right out of the door our plane had everything we needed, and we did not need clothes here we only wear white gauze clothes .

Hawaii

We walked to the landing strip and the pilots and stewardess were boarding with us. We went right to the bedroom to laugh and crack jokes about how we ditched our parents and left them babysitting. They didn't even realize what we did they were snoozing all over the babies they didn't care about us . Him go tup and continues working on the plane. I started working on the New Ginger and Spice Business. We have about 10 hours or so I will work diligently because I been slacking a lot, but it has all been worth it I thank the universe for my husband-kids-business-universal gifts-everything. The stewardess chimed in asking us what would we like for dinner. After listening to her choices, we both chose crispy fried Shrimp along with a sweet red.

When dinner was ready, we both came out and sat at the table to eat and while eating I looked at Him telling him how happy I am to have him then he looked up into my eyes and smiled then told me how happy he was to have me even with my craziness and we both started laughing. I was telling him that I never been to Hawaii and ever since I was a little girl I wanted to go to Hawaii, and he gave me my wish. He looked at me and then said candidly baby you are so sweet and the things that you say sometimes sound like BS, but I know your heart and know that you are being true. I opened my mouth to show him my chewed food then I kept eating when I looked up, he was staring at me then I told him that is my crazy side sometimes actions speak louder than words. He looked at me then said, " I love every little bit of you baby."

The pilot made the announcement that we will touch down in Hawaii in about 10 minutes I threw my hands in the air and moved my hips from side to side and screamed Hawaii YAYYY! All he could do was laugh with me.

SURI & HIM

Everything was set up so beautiful btu he was serious that were we were on this island it was just him and I and the people offering services only show up at that time. After the people set everything up for us, they left then he turned to me and asked me to turn off my cellphone then he continued to tell me that from time to time we have to get away from Wi-Fi running through our bodies-cellphones staring in our third eye and eyes. I looked at him in agreement then I thought about our kids being there with Wi-Fi running through their bodies. He laughed then said we will bring them and the boys soon but for now we need this baby. Then eh handed me the Itinerary and it was nice but then he told me how we would hunt for our fruit from the trees and live earthly and he want to teach me about trees-ocean- then I could not find my shoes he told me that no shoes will be worn here either so we can get all we need from the earth naturally. I asked him could anybody see us right now he shook his head no then I took off all my clothes he started laughing I told him how I wanted to know what did it feel like to just be naked he was laughing then I asked him to take off all his clothes he looked at me and told me that he will keep on his t shirt but can't be fully naked. I walked towards the water then yelled well you don't know what you are missing babies. He started running towards me and I ran into the water but stopped at my knees noticing how clear and beautiful the water was. He went ahead of me and held my hand as we walked all the way in until I dropped down, but I held onto his neck as we floated. The time we spend together is always so perfect I looked at him after kissing him and told him how happy I was that I have him now at this time in his life when he is seasoned, and he had his fill of women. He looked at me and made this noise like hmmmm. I looked at him and said hmmmm is right.

SURI & HIM

When we got out of the beach water and walked onto the sand, he put his arm around me and said even though this is a private part of the beach then we approached our cabin walked in he handed me this gauze thin white dress then told me to never ever do that again because there are always eyes and never forget that. I walked over to the door and peeked out and when I turned around, he smirked at me. After we bathed, I put on another one of the same dress and I heard him call me and when I turned the corner, he was sitting on the floor on his knees with candles all around. It looked so ritualistic he reached for my hand so I sat down In front of him, and he said to me this is how we will meditate morning and night I looked behind me and there was no wall just the ocean and the sound of the waves washing up close to our cabin. Right away my mind started to travel thinking that he was going to kill me soon and when I opened one eye to look at him, he had both of his open and he touched my head then he smiled and whispered to me " I would Never hurt a hair on your head" then I forgot we were supposed to be meditating and I said out loud or you know what I can do to you if you do he shushed me then out his finger to his lips then he laughed silently.

I could not believe this man had me meditating for a whole hour sheesh . We got up and he kissed me then he guided me to the bed outside for us to sleep . I looked at him and asked him could he protect me because I haven't seen him fight yet he only used his mind. He sat up on the bed and said trust me I can really fight I looked at him and said all I really know is that you better beat them up because while you fight imma be screaming Babies kick his ass. He laughed then reached for me and held me close in a spooning position then whispered, " Sweetheart after meditation you supposed to eb calm not loud and boisterous." I looked back at him and in a whisper, I said, "Oh I forgot Babies with my eyes squinched." Watching the sun go down felt unrealistic and so serene. I slept like a baby without a care in the world. He always made me feel like his property at all times like I am made of the most expensive glass the world makes that if broken could never be replaced. I know that even if he get so mad at me, he slap me then he would still get a pass because I know he love me.

SURI & HIM

When I woke up, I kissed him all over his face because he look so peaceful and kissable, he took his arms and stretched them over his head then opened his eyes and I pointed to the sun going up. It was so picturesque just breath taking. I sat up on the side of the bed watching the sun slowly rise then he sat up with me holding me in his arms and we both just sat quietly and watched.

He walked inside and brought back two empty backpacks and he took my hand then we started walking I could not believe this man was serious he was taking me to go look for food " Yep he is crazy." Well, he did go dig for my ring out the dirt so this shouldn't surprise me, but I don't know what lesson this is. He answered me out loud and said " The way the world is going baby you need to know how to hunt and find food ". Next, I have to teach you how to sign I said as in sign language he said yes because there has been a shift in the world where your words that you speak are as so. I said really so then he cut me off and said but the bad words and thoughts are favored so not talking at all but knowing how to communicate when it is needed. I was walking behind him while shaking my head he told me "Relax" . I said easier said then done he said, " Oh Please stop " I said ok then he said, " Please Don't Worry." I said ok fine I squatted down to pee up against a tree he stood there with his hand on his hips and said " you just did that " I said" I am doing it look at my stream" he said " Yep Suri is being Suri " we laughed.

We walked to this part, and he pointed to show me these plums then he told me that they were called "Java Plum" we picked some then Mangos-Macadamia nuts-Mountain apples-some edible plants even. We filled our backpacks then started walking back to our cabin then I said to him that I could not wait to eat dinner he just laughed so I stood in front of him and said " No way" he laughed and pointed to my backpack. When we returned, I sat down empties my backpack on the table . He took a bowl and washed them all off. I just sat quietly and ate the fruit and just decided to not talk to him for the rest of the night this was Ludacris. I did not know that my last meal would eb the last one on the plane if so, I would have stuffed my face.

SURI & HIM

Later that night we were laying in the bed, and he rolled over on top of me lifted my dress over my head he took his arm and reached under me to lift me up to him just right so he could kiss me. I wasn't going to give him some but this arm behind my back and lift up was different, so I just went with it. He reached over and reached under his pillow and pulled out these two beautiful flowers. He put one in my hair and the other one he put in his mouth then while still holding em up form my back his mouth met mines with the flower in it then I bit the middle of the flower it was a stem in it then he took his part and put it back on the bed then he kissed me while we shared the stem then he whispered to me ' This is a Hibiscus Flower." I smiled and then said to him WOW! In a soft whisper all stary eyed. he took his arm and turned me over it was so fast but not head spinning then laid me on my belly and turned my head to the side then started licking my neck and kissing then he followed my spine all the way down to my tail bone at the top of my crack then he laid on top of me I turned to look at him to tell him that I was a virgin he smiled then whispered, " I am your husband." I said yes you are right so ok just go slow. He started going slow, but he did not know he was inside of my vajayjay, but I went with it because I was tight enough for him not to know. I went with it without thinking it knowing he would find out and in a few minutes, I could feel his breathing on the back of my neck then I knew it was all over. I will keep this secret as long as he don't know. He turned me over to go and kiss my sweet spot, but I stopped him and told him I was tired form the hiking we did and just want to go to sleep. Then I went to the bathroom and was laughing so hard I had to turn on the facet of water so he could not hear me. This is the first time I have lied to him oh well nobody is always honest in life. My little butt hole could not take that horse cock he got no thanks. Well, he hasn't earned that yet one day I will but no time soon. This I will fake it till I do it. He knocked on the door to check on em I came out smiling then he went in.

SURI & HIM

It was Thursday I was still eating the fruit from the trees. He set up a table on the beach for two with a white tablecloth two lit candles and then I saw two women bring a huge box of cooked lobsters and wine it was dusk. So romantic. The ladies left and we went to sit down and eat. He was talking to me telling things about him I never knew like places he been-people he met-things he experienced he even told me that in another place there is a vagina museum that he loves, and he want me to go there with him so I can learn about how powerful a vagina really is, but he told me not to look at it from a sexual standpoint only from a science standpoint. I looked at him and said ok. I was so interested in him. Sometimes I pinch myself because I can't believe my husband is someone who I used to watch on television who I was afraid of for a long time. Then he looked at me with his eyebrows together and asked me why was I afraid of him. I started tearing up in my eyes then he sat back in his chair. He handed me a napkin to wipe my eyes. I was so choked up that I could not talk for a while I started looking out at the sea. He was staring at me just watching my thick tears run down my face. Every time I started to talk the words could not come out even my throat was full of tears. Then I had to vomit, and I threw up all the lobster and he said, " Well damn baby am I that bad?" I smiled a little and shook my head no. He asked me should he be concerned over what I am about to tell him I sat back down and shook my head no, but I still sat there quietly he reached for the glass of wine to drink some and patiently waited until I got myself together to explain why.

When we met online, I really didn't know if it was you, but I was innocent really just wanting you to take a picture with my twins because of their acting career. I did have those boxing gloves of yours, but you were never my dream to be my man nor was I a screaming fan when I was younger. You and your family ran a huge game on me, and you knew I was abused badly from sexual-metal-vocal. I was always trying to do right by my abusers, and I finally broke free from the sexual abuse by age 12 raped at 15 when my virginity was taken. I always had a smile on my face and remained happy. One thing for sure I told you all of this in the beginning of our friendship and when I tried to break free from you then you told me I was into o deep and manipulated me even your family -friends did it to em too they watched me and did me so bad then you put that thing in my uterus when we finally linked up. How could you do that to me and when I helped you do all this, and you used me this took time from my life and in the meantime, I lost my daddy and I saw how it all went down. I was threatened to lie by strangers. Different men on my cellphone. Listening to me then coming around me. You ruined my life and I forgive myself and you for what you did to me then you thought I did not know about all of what you did to me-my kids and family then your family let a grown woman have sex with one of my teen age sons. But I understand I have to forget about all that one thing I remember was asking you to please leave me alone soon as I saw the shit start, but you threatened me about things you knew I did when I was little. Then you wanted me to forget what I saw but you stayed away form me watching everything I did. So, I did you a favor to save your life and career. When I got away and was living my happy life working for the Suren's you came back, and you think I can mentally just put all you did to me away. Well, my son is in love with the older girl that is posing as a teenager I see all of how my life and family life was compromised but remember my job was to just stay happy and not complain but it never went away. All of my money was taken away from me that was you and your ex that did it and you know women they really get you . I tried to leave you in the beginning, but you kept it going and threatened me because you taped into my life and learned about everything, I ever did then used it against me if I left. Until this day you will tell me that it was not you, but I know you knew something about it. So, you wanted me so you would be king because that is what rich men do, they only know how to elevate and don't give a fuck who they smash along the way. I hope you got a lot because you ruined my life and my whole entire family, I remember the words " My family is worth more than yours" that is what was told to me to be exact.

I have always had respect for you and who television have shown you to be but as long as you can live knowing that you threatened and ran a game on me to be with me and let me tell you one last thing . When you came to me, and you showed me that porno of you fucking that deaf girl then that is why I fucked that old nigga with the uncircumcised dick that could not get hard. That was a helluvah experience. Then you blamed me of that when I did it thinking this will make it all go away and I would be left alone but you kept the game going and going. That is what sick people do so yes, I am now married to my worse abuser, so I have to make the best of it because you have changed so since you are the star, and I am a peasant I have to accept that because if I don't for the rest of my life I have to deal with bullshit and my boys too.

Thank you for meditating and the fruit it brought back some of the things I want to say to you. This is why death don't bother me and this is why Nikel dies she was that part of me that people did so wrong, and she always smiled with the same people and understood the WHY? But nobody ever really gave a fuck about her WHY? So, it is the same with me and I get it.

SURI & HIM

    YOU TOOK TO LONG and do your research a heavenly person like me don't need meditation they need people to stop taking them for fucking granted and to leave them alone if they don't mean them well. This is why I can be alone and had reservations about fucking with you even though all that shit is over at least I think it is , and You are OK I just have to forget about it and deal with it right. Well ok then I started smiling crying and eating my food. I looked at him and he was crying but he is a celeb they know how to instant cry so I just know that I was put here on earth to endure people's bullshit this is why when I do die I only want my twins at my first set of twins Aden and Amir at my funeral because I know that they really love me and for everyone else even my second set of twins they will be conditioned mentally by Him so they will be cold hearted as he is I will love them but I don't think they will be raised in a loving manor they will be like him. They will do whatever it takes to stay relevant .

    When we get back home, I need to go back to my condo for a while you can keep the twins, I will pump enough breast milk for them. Also, I will send breast milk by the twins to the castle to you. I am not upset with you I just need time the meditation made me remember that's all. Lastly, I know you want me to focus on GOD and I do but when I get all deep into GOD then your people be in my phone waiting for me to send me messages and a bunch of bad shit trying to do to me telling me be godly and listen. I will be throwing all my shit away when I get back .

SURI & HIM

I LOVE YOU SO MUCH but there is a time limit, and you took to long you never came back when the smoke was clear you took things to the next level so . Now since I meditated, I took things to the next level. Also, every time I used to play the lottery, I would watch that spirit following me make sure I did not get a winning ticket like I said I can see all the shit . Then when I got with you, I hit the lottery because you made my life a living hell and took all my money from me until I di what you wanted me to do. I broke away from you and you came back, and I let you in. Meditation is not for everyone, so you did this not me I remember the shit.

I know that I preach about love and it's all about love and I DO LOVE YOU, but I need you to understand the damage that was done that I had forgotten about. This World we live in Need Love but do people really know the damage they do to others when all they have to do is LOVE.

He got up reached over the table and grabbed me then he got up and walked to me while he was crying loud like a baby, I could hear all the hurt and pain from the inside of him. He started crying and telling me how sorry he was, and he could never let me go because he fell in love with me from the start it was just the wrong time and then he said that he knew that in order to have me he had to do something different because I was so special to him. He was leaning on me so hard crying that when I stepped back, we fell on the sand he kept crying it was so loud full of pain and anger he was screaming crying beating his hand in the sand telling em he was so sorry and to please forgive him. I tries to move but he pinned me under him and kept screaming and I could hear so much pain he was releasing while screaming begging me not to leave him and he will do whatever I need him to do in order to make this all go away from us.

SURI & HIM

    To see a calm man cry and let loose is a horrible site. I stood up and was just standing there watching him cry. I told him that I forgive him he sat up on his knees and reached over to hug me at my waist crying telling me how much he loves me, and he never wanted to hurt me or my family.

    When we washed up and went to sleep both our eyes were puffy and we looked horrible. The next morning when we woke up, we both looked like we had the fight of our lives I know that we both will need to wear shades for a while. I might have been too hard on him, but he never really told me sorry he just let it go hoping I guess I would forget and let it go but this outburst that he just went through gave me just what I needed to know that he was genuinely sorry. He laid on top of me and kissed me then started telling me how much he loves me, and he will fight till the death for our love. I told him how much I love him too then I asked him was it ok for me to put my guards down and to trust everything 100% going forward between us. He said yes baby. Then he asked me to please love our twins like you love Aden and Amir. I told him we have to raise them to be loving it is very important.

Suri's Dinner with Him

It was our last night together, so I had to make it special especially after what happened between us last night, we both had a good release. I got up early so I could get things together for us. After I got everything together, I woke him up with my famous kisses all over his sleeping face. He stretched then opened his eyes and smiled at me with the both of us having bubble eyes. I sat with him and asked him could we pray by the ocean, and I told him that I will meditate with him again when we get home maybe it was the environment why all that came up and out of me again. He got right up, and we held hands then walked over to the beach then we faced one another, and he led us into prayer. His words were beautiful.

We shared a piece of fruit together then I sat up and was looking at my thighs touching and squeezing them then he joined me then kissed each thigh telling me how beautiful my thigs were and how much he loves my soft body . I laid on him and then asked him could I invite him to a special dinner with me I felt his stomach shake a little like he was holding back a laugh. I looked up at him he looked down at me then he started tickling me then I did it back and realized that he is very ticklish OH WOW! We actually sat there tickling each other.

It was in the evening, so I walked over to the sand opened up a huge blanket it was shaped like a circle. I had our last piece of fruit and I put it in a bowl. Then I went back to lay down with him. I started singing to him I could sing since I was two years old, but I never had a person or people other than my twins who loved to hear me sing but now I go ta husband who totally loves to hear me sing so I stood up in the bed and started singing some oldies, but goodies songs and he would join in with me or correct my words from time to time. I just love him so much.

SURI & HIM

I forgot that we would be out at dusk for my dinner, so I went inside to get the beach torches stuck them down into the sand far away from us but close enough for us to get enough light. When it was time, I reached out for his hand and then we walked over to the blanket I told him to sit down first then I sat on my knees next to him and untied his pants to put him in my mouth focusing n the tip which is his heart until it became rock hard then I stood up and sat down on it, but I did not move. I asked him to take my legs and help me place them behind his back. I asked him was he okay with this he smiled then said yes, I am . Then I asked him could I do my 100 Kegels with him inside of me just trying something different he smiled and said of course you can. I started with my first Kegel along with pushing my pelvic floor down onto his hard on and he took a deep breathe but he was cool . I started talking to him while doing my Kegels I started telling him how I felt about his past. I rapped my arms around him and moved a little bit he looked into my eyes with the look of pleasure all over his face I started telling him that I know that people can be very jealous and might wan tot tell me about things that you did in your past or even show me evidence but I now your heart and I know their heart because they are being mean by telling me things about you to make me leave you but it will only put us closer together. I DON'T GIVE A FUCK ABOUT YOUR PAST I ONLY GIVE A FUCK ABOUT OUR PRESENT. I love us together we a good luck and the way we make each other feel is magical he said in a low voice " tell me about it I feel magical right now." I started twirling my hips really slow while doing my Kegels and pushing down my pelvic floor and he reached around to my back and started pushing me down more until he finished, I did not get up because like I told him I had to do 100 Kegels and I was up to number 25. He was sitting up on his arms then he held his head back because the after feelings of a good orgasm makes everything extra sensitive. When I got to 50, he had another orgasm but this time I squeezed a little harder and leaned back to really pull his dick and then I moved my sweet spot in a rhythmic motion then he put my nipple in his mouth through my gauze dress my whole tit fit inside of his hand . When he did that, I started to have an orgasm that I could not control so I leaned all the way back then he looked down to watch his dick go inside and out of me. Now I am at 75 this time I sat up placed my hand on the back of his neck and started moving front and back with me inside of me and with now soft fat ass he looked like he was in heaven enjoying all of his wife. Then I told him to count with me in a slow whisper but hold his orgasm until we get to 100 and at 100 while we orgasm lets say out loud all the good things, we want in our life I started with my Kegels and we started counting and when we got to 98 I lifted one of my legs onto his shoulder then he pulled me onto his dick until we both stared to orgasm and at the same time we wished for great health-prosperity-love-and a forever marriage. That is how we manifest sexually.

SURI & HIM

    After we finished, I could barely walk he helped me up and we went to lay back down on the bed . When we laid down, he started whispering in my ear telling me how much he loves me, and he is so sorry he hurt me then he told me how he never had a woman like me before and every time we have sex it is very creative and in my small voice I said, and I will always be that way and keep you guessing about what's next. He looked at me with this funny look and said " tell me about it ".

    I went to get our bags and make sure we had everything in them, and I realized that when he get back on the plane int eh morning our cellphones will be pinging away. I started telling him how I knew my mother would be showing up at the castle because she want to be hands on with all her grandchildren. He told me that he knew his mother was wondering too. I said My mother definitely has a problem with me leaving Lizzy in charge of the twins when we go places. We both laughed about them. I turned around and asked him what did he think about us moving our mothers in the castle to help with the twins. They will not be alone and then we could have freedom and not worry about the babies when we need to take care of business and not always leave them on Lizzy. He told me that he would think about that because remember you said that " There is ONLY ONE QUEEN IN YOUR CASTLE." I looked at him with squinted eyes and said, " Why you have to Quote me" That was who I was then not now I am sure they both understand who is Queen of the Castle but I will let you decide baby and whatever you say that is what it will be My King.

    After packing we both went to sit on the beach and listen to the waves, He laid his head on my lap then he asked me about all the keys I knew about I looked down and told him that if I told him I would have to kill him then I laughed he looked at me and laughed with me. Then I said baby all I can tell you right now is that all of us here on earth are not alone everyone have spirits hanging with them at all times. We just can't see them, but they damn sure see us. He sat up and said " Suri they see you and all those things you do to me" being facetious then I said " they sure do, and I know they be holding their mouth but that's me and they shouldn't stop my fun because YOU ARE MY HUSBAND. He shook his head and said yep, I agree with you and don't you ever stop. Then he got serious and asked me why in the beginning did I just lay there every time we had sex. I laughed at him and said because I knew you was dishing out big bullshit and I wasn't about that, so I made you do all the work but look at us now wasn't it all worth it babies.

SURI & HIM

    I can tell you something else about the world and it's climate right now. Everybody has to pay for things that they have done to others and if you have made right with what you have done to someone then now you have to mind your business while you watch people receive their karma no matter who they are and if you intervene in their karma then you are singing up for their karma to be given to you and off of them. I know so much babies and the more keys that are given to me I am learning to just sit and watch this shit. One thing for sure I believe in GOD that is how I was raised so that's all I know because I am a creature of habit, but I also know about them .

    If people can't, see that we have to forget about this race shit and live life and black woman can make many changes to be better but that is up to them, and I am not sure if they are willing to work on becoming a Suri. I am not perfect at all, but I am not that bad babies. I don't have all the answers but from what I have been trusted with I know I am minding my own business because you can't tell humans nothing. I just have to protect my husband-kids- and those who listen to me but the first time I talk facts to you, and you keep talking out the side of your face about some shit you saw on social media then I just smile and agree but like I said being a 113 is not easy when you have to deal with people and even my kids when they get to a point where they know everything then what can a person do. Then I look around and hear people talking about slavery, but I believe all races have had difficulties in the past some worse than others, but we all bleed red blood. We will never forget about the harsh times of our ancestors, but shouldn't we be grateful that it wasn't us that had to go through that I know I am grateful. So, the question is how can we move forward as people and help one another instead of hurting one another because one person is better than the other or can do more than the other what about joining those who are great and learning from them if they let you in to learn and if not still wish then the best in life. This is why I have no friends-love to be home- you can go out whenever you want, and you don't have to take me with you I want you to go out and have fun with your friends and never worry about me not going out I am not made to be out and around people like that I just need friendly acquaintances not friends because I carry something to were people don't like me after a while.

SURI & HIM

I have finally learned about my happiness I just found out that if I do what I want it feels better and I will never people please again no matter how harsh I come across.

I got spirits who follow me throughout my day that shit sucks but whatever. Then he looked up at me and he wiped the tear that ran down my cheek. Then I continued about how cruel things were done to me by my family and I watched it all and as a matter of fact still watching it but they will not listen to me so I have to sit back and watch it all but the people doing it to them will never have me for themselves or their family.

After my long winded conversation, I looked down to tell him that I have heard many people say that I talk to much but that one time I became quiet people ruined my fucking life and I have to be silly as fuck and wear a smile in order to get through something that is still going on and the worse thing of all the people doing it are black people-black women- my won people .All I can Say to that is "GOD BLESS AMERICA".

He sat up then looked at me and with his authoritative voice he said, " Suri stop with the bullshit tell me about the keys you are so good at throwing words all around and your storied be so good a person can drift right into your words and the tone of voice you use.' Then he said, " baby I am waiting." I stood up and wiped the sand off my body then I stood in front of him and nervously said " Ok I will tell you, but you have to wait and let me do something first . He sat with his lips twisted looking like he was thinking " Here we go again with the antics." I stood in front of him and then I started walking backwards he started laughing I kept walking when ocean got to my feet, he got quiet then I kept going until the water got to my neck then I took a deep breathe and backed up until it covered my head, and I held my breath. I always could sing long notes so I knew that I could hold my breathe very long. Then I fell because he rushed into the water when he did not see me anymore. He lifted me out of the water, and I started laughing telling him that I needed to clear my mind before I share with him the keys. When we got back to the blanket, he was pissed but I was laughing at him. I guess he does love me he came to save my life.

I stood back up my gauze dress was wet clinging to my naked body and all my curves, and he was looking me up and down, but I ignored that because he wanted to know what the keys were, and I knew that I could never tell him all of them that is the universal law along with him having to search and find the keys on his own.

SURI & HIM

I wanted to stall him, so I started shaking my hips and rapping I said :

So, Listen Imma drop some scripts from my lips no dissin

Watch me shake my hips take a dip

Then go sippin

The words that I say sound cray

And you know I talk so much it will take all day

So many people prey on knowledge and wisdom

But what they don't know is it starts with them

First thing first to start this verse

Imma take my time to rock this rhyme

The birds and the bees the leaves on the trees was the first message given

For all of us to succeed.

When I stopped, he had the nerve to tell me to keep gong while he chuckled laughing. I stopped then dropped down in front of him out of breathe. He reached for my hand helped me up the n he said " baby I will wait until you give me the keys you want me to have, and I will search for my keys on my own. I slapped him on his bottom with my free hand then tried to run and he ran pass me so fast and left me in the dust as they say. When I made it to him, I told him that I know that he couldn't possibly like that rap. I be messin around and after I said that we looked at each other then he aid " baby remember when we used to mess around, I laughed then said yes baby do you want to mess around again he said not really, I am enjoying the real deal. I smiled then said me too babies.

SURI & HIM

    We boarded our plane around 9 am in the morning and soon as the stewardess asked what would we like for dinner. I told her give the both of us 4 servings a piece of whatever she got. When the food came, I stuffed my face I was so hungry and since we had a long time until we get home, I ate all that food then went to sleep with a nice full belly.

    When we walked into the house Lizzy was there of course we asked for our kids, and she pointed into the Livingroom and our babies were standing up by themselves along with our mothers teaching them. They actually loved their grandkids, and they were enjoying one another's company, We walked over to the kids and gave them kisses and hugs then we took them to our room with us and told our mothers to enjoy the castle do whatever they want. I heard them call Lizzy and I think Lizzy been hanging out with them in the castle now that was sweet.

    We both took the twins and laid them in between us just looking at them smiling and growing so fast. I told him that I want to Wien them off of my breasts and give them yellow Gatorade diluted with water and a liquid infant vitamin. He looked at me like I was bonkers then I laughed and told him that my first set of twins could not drink any milk at all so the doctor had no choice, and we gave them just that Gatorade diluted with water and vitamins and trust me they grew so smart and healthy and look at them today they are smart oh might I add that they did not eat food until age 2 and sweets until they were older. He sat to think for a minute then he agreed with me. SO, I pumped my breasts for one more month, but a lot was stored in bags int eh fridge then we slowly started with the Gatorade.

    It was 2 in the afternoon, and I seemed to be still tired like I needed to rest more so I went to go lay down. Him came into the room telling mt that he had to leave and had a meeting in midtown today. I told him Good Luck and Be safe. He came over to me and kissed me then he left. I was so comfortable with the covers pulled up over my head then I drifted off into sleep and started dreaming.

SURI & HIM

The Dream:

I was walking in Manhattan shopping I saw a store called "Nikel's" So if course the store name interest me so I walked in, and it was like a boutique so I started looking at the clothing and items they had and when I turned around Nikel was standing there, she told me to come sit on the chair in the boutique so she could tell em some things that I needed to know. She smiled at me then she told me how proud of me she was and to never tell Him all of the keys because he has to find and search for him own, and she said how trusting that I am also I have to learn how not to be even with my husband because he has to pass tests in order to be trusted and I will know when to tell him. So, I leaned close and whispered tell him what. She laughed at me and said " Gurl you have spirits who follow and protect you and this is one of the keys." I said wait so it is true that they see me having all that good sex then we both laughed while she shook her head yes. I told her could she tell them to close their eyes because I am not gonna stop having sex with my husband. She said I did not have to, but she wanted me to know. I asked her could they stop following me she told me that they been there by me since I was a little girl, so they are used to being around. Then Nikel said but like when you want them to protect your family you can ask them to follow them, and they will. You are blessed to have this just keep on being sweet. Then she took out a piece of paper for me to read and it was information for me to write a book for women. I shook my head ok then I went to reach for her, and I woke up.

SURI & HIM

The covers were thrown all over the floor like she wanted me to know that the dream was real because my covers stay on me especially when I am on bed alone, I tuck my covers under my body.

I got up to go look for my babies and when I went downstairs the ladies were in the kitchen cooking-talking- the babies were in baby chairs siting listening to them. Christopher was walking by, and I looked at Chris and he waved his hands looking happy Lizzy had some friends to talk to and I was loving how our mothers were getting along. I sat down at the table to drink some coffee-play with my babies and listen to tall the latest information about teas-knee remedies-HBP-pains- GOSH! That is a lot to go through when you age so this is why you supposed to live your life then they asked me what did we want to eat for dinner today. I text and ask him he told me to decide so I told the ladies they can decide so whatever they want to cook. As I was texting to ask him, I could see all of their eyes were on me like I was doing something wrong. I know this topic will come up with them so I will just wait on it.

My email sent me a notification and when I opened the email it was from a VP of a company interested in me using their spices for the "Ginger and Spice with Everything Nice LLC." They want to meet with me for dinner today. I stood up and started doing dance looking at my phone. I kissed my babies and left to go get my clothes ready. I have to meet them in midtown by 7pm tonight. I walked into my closet looking around I noticed that all my clothes were new again so felt like I was in a store. I was bending over, and I felt a slap on my ass it was Him I stood up fast and turned around we laughed. I told him about my meeting then he took his phone and told me that I have to let security drive=wait-bring me back home . I told him ok He was telling me that he will eat dinner with the ladies today including Lizzy. I smiled at him and said now that will be nice. I reached for my long thick silk teal wrap Dress down to my ankles. I know that there is one ghost who follow me and sometimes he stops my luck he has a jealous spirit but its fine. I ignore him and am not afraid of him. I found away to think without being heard and I will never disclose that key to Him. One of the things I learned from my daddy is that when you got some shit going on in your life you have to get to the root of it and it may cause you to look crazy-say and do crazy things unlike your character and never be afraid to die along with keeping your mouth shut so I be sillay not silly sillay and so far, they just think I am naive-silly-not that smart. "It's All A Game Taught TO Me By My Daddy."

SURI & HIM

    I entered the restaurant and as I saw the phones go up some trying to sneak a few pictures, but it was fine. My security detail walked inside of VIP with me so they can check the area and to get a look at who I was meeting with then they walked to stand in front of the place then I got a text that one of them noticed a back door so they will stand by that door . I said ok then I looked up to meet the women and they started setting up their spices and telling me where they originated from. There was another VIP table behind us with a bunch of men talking business. I kept my back turned but I was ear hustling while I was talking and taking care of my own business. The ladies had beautiful spices that smelled delicious.

    My ears became extra sensitive to listen when I heard one of the men say, " If Black Women only knew." So, I wanted to turn around and ask, " Knew What?" but I had to keep listening. Then the waitress came over to me for my order then to the men, so she broke the conversation. I was so nosey that I wanted to know so bad what black women should know. So, the women at my table started placing a bunch of spices in these glass jars each one labeled for me to try for 30 days then let them know if I want to do business with them. Then they got up excused themselves as they walked out my food was coming towards me. So, I started reading their brochure while I ate then I got a text from security asking em if I was ok, I told them yes and I am going to finish my dinner before we go back.

SURI & HIM

So, then the conversation continued with the guys asking what was he talking about? Then he continued saying that he received a mental download about black women and part of the New World Order was turning black women against one another because they have the gifts to rule the world and you know they and out of my peripheral I saw him point up . He said they would never let that happen because when they get in positions of power, they get nasty to everyone from their man-kids-and they get to bougie now not all but such a high percentage that it's too much for black men. So, what brings me to what I want tell you is that would a black woman really want to know what number their pussy fall on when it comes to premium pussy. The other men were quiet just looking at him. Then he continued that women of different nationalities they know the value of their pussy and they know that when you add a black man to their life their value goes up just like his value go up sometimes but Black women could shoot to number one if they can fix their ways because the value of pussy got a lot to do the sweetness of the woman-how she loves a man and more but in 2022 I sit back and watch the destruction of the black woman see a black man have it hard but he will always get him a woman even if he a mean dude but the black woman have some cleaning up to do and guess what I was watching this show were this one girl was being mean to the other and when she asked why are being so mean to me the girl said as she walked away " This is The New World Order". I said ohhhh Shit! The attack is on ruining the black woman against herself-her man- other black women and as strong as we are supposed to be how we let this happen and it is out of a black mans control at this point.

I was on my way home and all I could think about was numbers 1-100 and were a black woman rank at and that guy did not even share that. I probably would have choked on my food especially knowing that there are values to different nationalities of pussy. When we pulled up Him was standing there to open the car door, he reached in to take the heavy bag of spices. He touched my butt again and I looked back at him and giggled. I walked in the house and the ladies were at the bar I looked at him because I knew he had them partying it looked like they were having so much fun together.

SURI & HIM

    I started getting undressed and looking at the twins sleep on the monitor then I jumped int eh shower. When I got out, he was in the chair reading so I sat in my chair then turned to him and asked him to please be honest with me because I need to know this, and you are a man so I know you will tell me. He smiled so I asked him does a woman nationality makes her pussy more valuable he leaned his head back and started laughing for a long time. When he stopped laughing, he asked me why did I ask him that so I told him about the men at the restaurant and then he said ok well I probably would say it is the same for men and woman and the value of anything is how it is presented from the outside in, but it really supposed to be the inside out. I said but the men were saying in other words on the pussy meter he would not even share where the black woman pussy is numbered. Then Him Laughed and said " WOW! A Pussy Meter are you serious?" Who said this? I said I don't know them, and I would not look at them.

    He took picked up his cellphone and then he waited, and I heard his phone ping he turned the phone around and it was a full video of me at my meeting then me listening to them. Him told me he knows the guys and they are a bunch of men who's out there doing the Community dick thing. They will grow pass that phase but anyway then I gave him mean eyes because I wanted to know about having me on video without my consent then he told me that I can sign the consent forms tomorrow, but I will always be in camera when I leave the castle especially alone then I asked do he be on camera. He smiled then said well not all the time because some of my meetings cannot be due to information baby and you know that. I said ok babes then I crawled over to him from my seat and softly made small bits between his leg holding him in between my teeth and like that he sat back and took it out and I put it in my mouth and was ravenous about it and he finished really fast. I work at being in tune with him and seeing how fast I could do it each time. I love getting to know my man's satisfaction's.

SURI & HIM

We went go lay down to go to bed then he looked at me and asked me did I want to know where I was on his meter. I looked at him confidently and said Nope because I know were I am already I got here in my bed every night right and to add on to you asking me this I am so sure of myself that any man I choose will always be satisfied. Then he sat up and said, "Suri you took that to far." I said no I didn't there are some questions you ask and some you don't so you asked you don't question because we both should know ere I am at. I kissed him and leaned into him all cuddled up and went to sleep and left his ass staring at the ceiling all night. I LOVE MY BABY and I know I can seem to be silly but trust and believe I KNOW WHO I AM.

I am not saying that she doesn't have to do her part, but The majority of Black Women want to be loved from the heart of their man and not to be bullshitted and not games be played on them also to be able to keep their guards down because he secured them to be able to be this way that is part of what a lot of it boils down too at least in my eyes, I Guess. Both the black man and Black woman need to put in work and also stop being with and marrying people for all the wrong reasons we can began there or when you see the relationship is not for you then it is time to move on and moving on is easy for the majority of men but for women it is harder. Whenever there is a spiritual aspect of the world like it is now, we have to hold on tight to one another in order to overcome and stand strong as we did years ago because we had no choice,

SURI & HIM

Him

  Suri through me for a loop just now because she is so sweet and all that good stuff but when she be serious that shit hit me in the middle of my chest because she never yells or get mad, she just get serious and uses this certain tone. She is so high vibing that when she get like this it feels fuckin spooky. She had a nerve to answer me in her sleep and say BOO! After I said spooky, I forgot she can hear me.

  I went to the gym and as I was sitting on the bench, I saw my headphones, so I picked up my player and started listening to music and thinking then something came to me about how to block listeners even Suri. So, I started thinking with the music on loud in my ears and I thought some really crazy things that would make Suri come and question me but instead I got a text from her asking me to please turn down my music so I knew then that she can't hear me if music is playing, I jumped up and started laughing and box punching the air I was so happy.

  I decided to take the time to think about our mothers moving in and helping with the twins. I can't let them move in, but they can help when we go away and come stay but other than that I want to raise my kids my way. I know that our mothers have their special ways and I welcome them, but I and Suri will have to keep our authority because I know what Suri is gonna say when her only daughter start to focus on her grandma and not Suri, I will always keep my kids on me knowing I am their daddy but with women it's different. Suri always wanted a daughter and she told me how when she was pregnant her mother would tell her that she need a son every pregnancy and that is what she had all boys in which she loves her kids but now I gave her a daughter and truth be told Suri can raise a Great woman so she doesn't' need no other females hands on her daughter to much or else I will hear it all day so I will let Suri know that our mothers would never move in with us but they can help us and if they don't like that then that's all I can extend. I will always step up for things that I now will not end up well it was like God gave us back our boy and girl and they both need us and to be raised by us they are different just like us.

SURI & HIM

My phone pinged and it was an incoming face call from Kevin so I sat up all sweaty and answered the call he was laughing and happy telling me that he has finished up and will be back home in 2 days and want to hook up to talk business as always . I asked him how was he really doing? He looked at me serious and said I am good man I am ok I can't wait to get home to start reading that book Nikel Left me. I thought he read that already he told me he did not because he had to get over what happened also, he needed his mind geared and focused on business now that he is coming back home, he has time to read. He invited us over to his place for a meeting then he asked could Suri get the buffet together. I pointed at him and said nah man you ask her he said btu she is your wife then I said but she also works for you that is between yall. I only pop up when Suri need that elbow work putting. Kevin started laughing then we hung up. I could hear Suri just talking nonstop and walking towards the gym I sat up to look at her walk in and I heard her say ok what kind of food then he said whatever you want just use the black card . Then Suri looks at me with this sexy look and said oooohhhh The black card of course I will. Then I said out loud " OK Kevin see you in two days." Then Suri looked at him then me with her mouth open and we both laughed at her. Then she came over to kiss me and said I was tryna make you jelly babies I laughed then told her that she could never do that because I am sure of me and very sure of her.

I told Suri how nice her body looks as she went to get on the Himsur Bike then she pointed to my spot motioning me to get on so I did then she asked me about our mother moving in and she had a whole fucking story production like really giving me the big picture and this and that I was just looking in her face as she explains like a kid would with eyebrows high-voice soft-lots of smiles then when she finished I waited then I said ok baby well are you ready for baby Suri to start calling your mother mommy by a mistake or wanting your mother more than you or then Suri put her hand up and she said hmmmm never thought about that then I kept talking and said well they can stay yes and when we go away they can come keep them of course but living here nope I have seen so many times when to many women live together sooner or later it just can't work unless the women know and stay in their place and I know my mother well and you know your mother so the only woman that knows her place is Lizzy. I am just giving you the view from the other side in which that is my job as your husband .

SURI & HIM

      Then She looked sat me and told me that I was correct then she looked away like she was thinking. So, I told her " A Million for Your Thoughts." She said Not a penny I said nope a million because. our thoughts are out of this world sometimes. She made a fake laughing scrunch face at me then she told me that the day she was in the kitchen and Lizzy asked what sis we want for dinner so I told them wait so I could text you then when I texted you then you answered right away, I told Lizzy but then when I looked up, they were all staring at me so I took that as they may fell like why I tell you everything even Amir girlfriend asked me the same thing. I smiled then said well, this is the way you like it I never asked you to be that way. Suri looked at me and said well, I am different, so I just have to get used to people thinking I am a fool for being this way with my husband. Then I told her, or they wish they were that way with their husband or maybe you are showing them something they feel they should do or have done btu next time they look at you ask them why and open the floor up for the conversation so then you will know exactly what they were thinking always know Suri that you never know how you touch or teach people but if you ask them, they WHY? In their action you will know the exact reason.

      Suri looked at me again and said see this is why I love you so much because you care about what I care about and if it is something that I might move to fast on you always bring me back to see things through a different lens. I looked at Suri and said Thank you, but you are one on a million that invest in her man as far as what he knows, and you always give me my place as A Man As YOUR MAN. There are so many married black men in this world and not the ones who are fucked up abusive and all that bad shit. I am talking about the decent black men many of them don't have a say so in their own home but then their woman wonder why they step out on them or is never happy with them they just existing in an unhappy relationship. Suri looked at me then said but there are always two sides baby I don't agree with anyone being unhappy I feel they should divorce or breakup because there is somebody for everybody and being robbed of happiness sucks. Just like I know if We opened the world up to see our sex life, they would probably call us freaks especially me because of all the sucking I do on you, but you keep yourself healthy and eat the right things so everything coming out of you taste good. I looked at her with my eyebrows together then said why you turning this into ta moment. She got off of the bike and said moment like what moment.

      I got off the bike and grabbed her by her ass then we kissed then she sat on this bench we have in the gym and opened her legs. I sat on the bench with her then our phone pinged it was Lizzy calling us to come downstairs and it was important.

SURI & HIM

We got up and ran downstairs and when we opened the doors to the club area the twins were dancing up and down to my music. I started laughing then Suri and I walked over to our babies and stayed downstairs watching them dance. Then we took them upstairs with us to our room in their walkers.

I asked Suri why doesn't she want to lead women or couples to help them . She looked at me then rolled her eyes. I laughed and asked her again and then she looked at me sat down int eh chair and said " Well, when it comes to helping women they have to know that they need and want the help because when anyone is able to use their power in their relationship to ruin-payback-use-misuse-treat badly- you know all of what I mean then they feel they are right because they see it makes the other person do what they want but it brings me to one of the keys well not really a key but when two people are in a relationship the way they treat the other is what they will get in the end like if a person always complain about their mate and act like they not together then in the end the person will get just that they will be old and alone because this is what they asked for while the person was in their life. The same amount of years they did this person that way they have to recuperate those years getting what they wished for. Thoughts and words really are things but everyone get their karma back I don't care how much you ask god for forgiveness he forgives you but you must be punished for what you did it and we call it karma which id good and bad so you have to choose what you want while you are dealing with people just be good and I don't know if I am ready to help because everybody can't be a Suri and that is my superpower.

Suri

I was thinking about Him telling me how I could be good for helping other couples or women but that is not what I want to be known as when I die because the truth is about the majority of human beings is we all know right from wrong, and I see a lot of things in relationships that a person can't say they did not know how what they did would affect the other and I don't have time for this world we live in I just have time for my household.

I used to have that Let Me Save The World Attitude but not anymore, it's just about those who are in my circle other than that I have learned to mind my business because what I see- What I know- and it's ridiculous.

WHAT THE WORLD NEEDS NOW IS LOVE, and I don't know if the world is too far gone to even achieve the love we want. I hope things turn around in this world soon.

The End

SURI & HIM

Thank you for supporting my dream. Keep your eyes open for my new nook "Love Language.

Made in the USA
Middletown, DE
26 October 2022

13583163R00029